For Debbie, her cousin Austin and Mrs. Okorah, who organised it all

First published in Great Britain in 2004 by
Frances Lincoln Children's Books, 4 Torriano Mews, Torriano Avenue, London NW5 2RZ
www.franceslincoln.com

Distributed in the USA by Publishers Group West

British Library Cataloguing in Publication Data available on request

ISBN 1-84507-047-X
Set in Myriad

Printed in China
1 3 5 7 9 8 6 4 2

Here Comes Our Bride!

An African Wedding Story

Ifeoma Onyefulu

FRANCES LINCOLN CHILDREN'S BOOKS

Introduction

In Africa, marriage is not just about the union of two people, but of two families. So it is important for each family to try to judge the strength of the other family by testing it out.

In this book, set in Benin City, in Nigeria – where my sister-in-law's family lives – the groom's family is given a list of things to do and a time limit for completing the tasks. How well Osaere's family tackles the tasks will indicate how successful the union is likely to be.

To cement their new friendship, the families often tease each other, which helps break the ice after the formality of the traditional meetings and tasks.

In this book, the groom's family asks to meet the bride, so, to heighten the excitement, a game of hide-and-seek is played: a cousin of the bride is hidden under a veil and presented as the bride. Of course, everyone roars with laughter when they discover they have been tricked! Eventually the bride is officially introduced to her new family, marking the beginning of their new life together.

After the traditional wedding, a church, mosque or even registry wedding is held, usually several months later.

I want to go to a wedding! All my friends have been to a wedding except me.

"Uncle Osaere, are you and Aunt Efosa going to get married soon?" I asked one day, when he came to our house.

"Wait and see, Ekinadose. Wait and see," he said.

I hate waiting!

Then last week, some people came to our house.

"We've come to see your grandfather," they said.

I took them into the parlour where Grandfather was.

Then I stood in the doorway listening.

Does this mean Uncle Osaere is going to get married?

Grandfather welcomed them, and my cousin Ado brought them drinks and kola nuts.

The oldest man in the parlour said a prayer and broke the nuts with his fingers. Then Ado passed round the pieces. Everyone ate and drank.

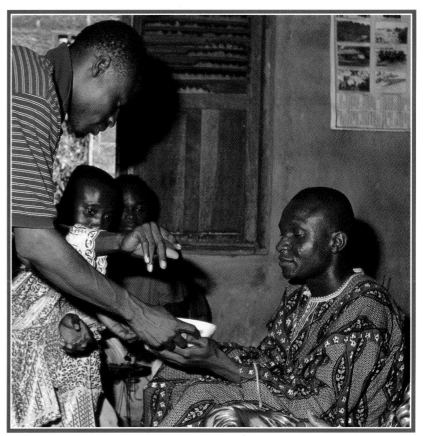

Kola nuts grow in pods on tall trees, and they keep for weeks after they have been picked. They represent friendship, harmony and peace between people. No one breaks a kola nut in front of his enemies — kola nuts bring people together.

One of the visitors said, "We have come today because of the young woman living in your household."

Is he talking about Aunt Efosa?

They all said Uncle Osaere was a good doctor from a good family, and was as strong and tall as an Iroko tree.

But when I heard the word *ugieoromwen* – which means 'marriage' – I asked, "Is Uncle Osaere going to marry Aunt Efosa?"

"Wait and see, Ekinadose."

I don't want to wait and see. I want to dress up for a wedding NOW!

The family of the groom-to-be try to impress their future in-laws by making formal speeches. It is like someone advertising his product in a busy market!

Grandfather said, "My granddaughter is a great woman, strong and wise beyond her years. She is an architect. And from a good family, too."

Everybody in the room cheered and clapped.

After everyone had finished talking, Grandfather asked one of my cousins to write down a list of things. Then he gave the list to the visitors to take away with them.

But nothing happened. I waited and waited for the people to come back.

A list of special things is given to the groom's family to put together, to test whether the groom can take care of the bride.

Then one day they did come back, and Uncle Osaere was with them. He brought gold necklaces and bangles for the bride.

Everyone showed the things they had brought: crates of beer and soft drinks, a bottle of schnapps, a calabash of palm wine, alligator pepper, kola nuts, yams and white envelopes with money inside. My cousins put them on the table for everyone to see.

Does this mean there's going to be a wedding?

It is most important that the groom-to-be's family brings everything on the list, because each item means something special. Alligator pepper has lots of seeds, which stand for fertility. The kola nut stands for peace and harmony and the schnapps are for our ancestors, who are invited to witness the union of the couple.

Everyone shouted, "We want to see our wife, our new wife!"

"Wife?" I said.

"Shhhh… Wait and see, Ekinadose, wait and see," everyone whispered again.

My mother and my aunt brought in a woman wearing a wedding dress, her head hidden under a cloth. One of the visitors took away the cloth and laughed.

"This is not our wife!" they shouted.

Then they brought in another person – but she wasn't the new wife either!

By now, everyone was laughing.

It was like the hide-and-seek game I play with my friends.

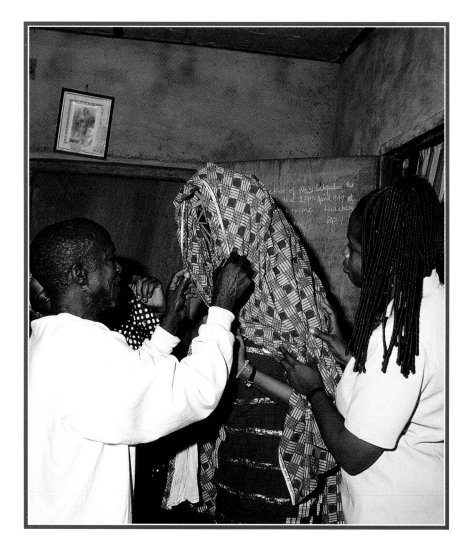

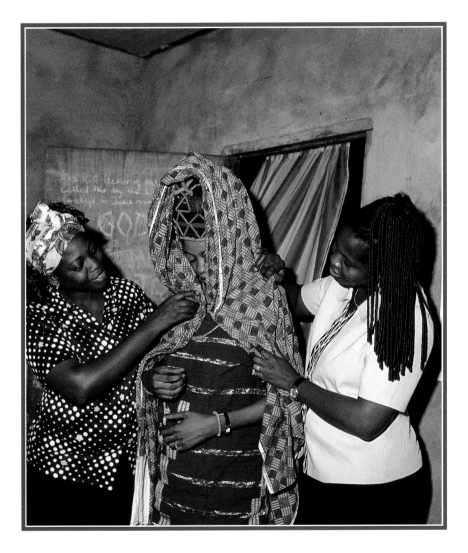

"We want our wife! Give us our wife!" everyone chanted.

"Yes – give them their wife! I can't wait any longer!" I said.

After a long time, my mother and my aunt came back and I saw someone else with them. She was hiding under a cloth, too.

"Not again," I said.

Slowly, very slowly, someone took the cloth off – and guess who it was? Aunt Efosa! She was wearing lovely clothes.

"Efosa! Efosa! Efosa!" everyone shouted.

Is she going to marry Uncle Osaere – is she?

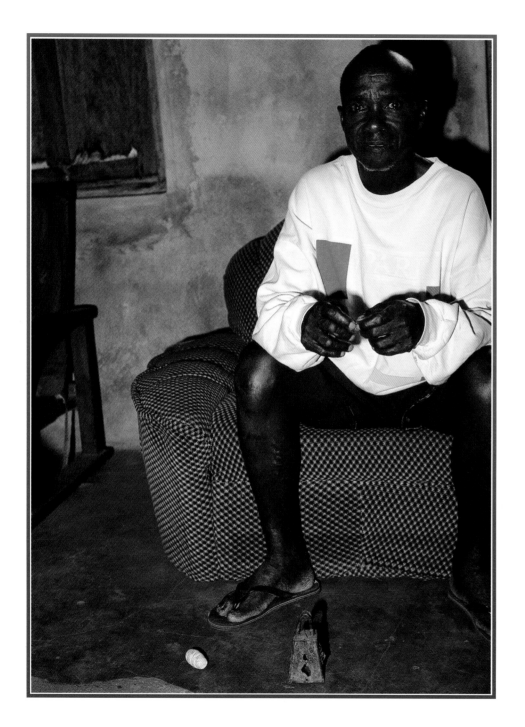

Later, an old man rang a hand-bell and drew some lines on the floor with a piece of chalk.

He said, "We ask you to witness the joining of our two children as husband and wife. Bless them and keep them."

He was talking to our ancestors.

He poured some schnapps on the floor for our ancestors to drink.

Then he passed the chalk and the schnapps
to Uncle Osaere and Aunt Efosa.

**We draw on the floor
to make a wish for the future.**

"They are now husband and wife!"
everyone shouted.

We started eating and drinking.
It went on all day long.
And guess what…?

There was another wedding after this one! The second wedding was in a church. This time Aunt Efosa wore a beautiful white dress and veil. She looked lovely, and so did Uncle Osaere in his best suit. It's the first time I've seen him looking lovely!

Some time after the traditional marriage, a wedding ceremony is held in a church, mosque or registry office according to the couple's religious beliefs.

I wore my best clothes – so did my sisters. They didn't seem to know anything about weddings, so I looked after them and showed them how to behave.

It was a good thing I did, because even more people came to the second wedding. There were musicians too. People danced until their legs ached.

Everyone was very happy. There were heaps of presents
for Uncle Osaere and Aunt Efosa. Then we ate lots of cake.

Now I can't wait for the next wedding.

I wonder who it will be… ?

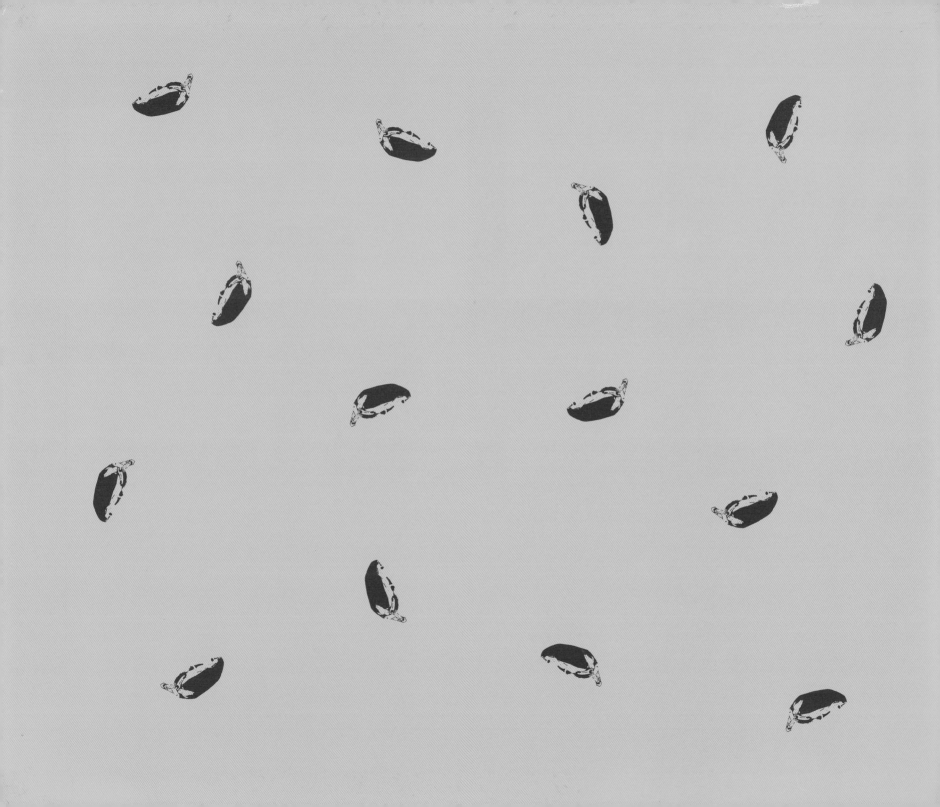